GOAL SETTING

Creating Change and Improving Performance

JOE BOONE

Copyright Notice

No part of this book may be reproduced or transmitted in any form whatsoever, electronic, or mechanical, including photocopying, recording, or by any informational storage or retrieval system without express written, dated and signed consent from the author. All copyrights are reserved.

Table of Contents

    Introduction

1   Defining a Goal

2   Behavior Change

3   The Support System

4   The Long Haul: Turning Motivation into Dedication

5   Habits of Performance

Introduction

This book came about because of my love for progression, at all levels. I believe that one of the keys to progressing is creating the appropriate conditions for the change you desire. Many people do not realize that what they do every day impacts them in the present as well as years from now. The realization that a change needs to occur for a healthier and higher performing lifestyle is a very powerful event, no matter where on the spectrum you fall.

In this book you will find some very easy and usable principles to apply in making any change. Many people already use some of these without even knowing it. The real power of these principles comes when you can manipulate them with a specific target in mind. A similar power comes when you transform a dream to an idea, as dreams have much more potential than we give them credit.

Dreaming is the first step to goal building. In this book I lay out some basic ways of thinking and strategies to act on to realize your dreams. The example I give is very simplistic, but is easy to apply to all areas of life. My goal is to provide you with the tools to succeed no matter the obstacle. When reading this text, open your mind to what I am saying and how it can translate to anything in your life.

So many times our lives are so busy that we lose focus on our goals. The purpose of this book is to show you how to take small things and transform them, ultimately giving you the tools to create big change and a life that all together becomes less burdensome, more enjoyable, and higher performing.

-Joe Boone

1

Defining a Goal

Setting a goal is a concept largely rooted in our psychology, and more specifically what we want out of life. Goals apply to our health, wellness, and fitness, and therefore all areas of life. Most goals are made because we dream. Maybe the dream was something so big that you would have never thought it a possibility. This is where psychology comes in. Sometimes people have a dream for themselves, but they don't even try for it because they think it's impossible. Instead of limiting yourself before you even begin, you must ask yourself, why isn't it possible?

Do you dream of losing two hundred pounds? Do you dream of lifting two hundred pounds? Do you dream of walking into the room and having people stare at you, recognizing the hard work you are putting in? Do you dream of breaking all of people's expectations? All of those dreams will become a reality, if you work toward your goals.

To successfully transform a dream in to a goal or set of goals it has to become focused. Maybe that big picture isn't attainable right this second, but it can and will be reached if you set the appropriate conditions. Open your mind to the option that one day you will be able to make it happen. Imagine you dreamed that you were your idol. That seems like an unattainable feat, but if you break it up in to different sets of goals it becomes more and more attainable. That person is a human just like you, and if they can do it that means that they had a dream that they transformed into a reality, just like you can in any goal if you build it correctly.

Developing a goal or goal set is a crucial part of the process of achieving optimal life performance. Life performance is achieved by creating the appropriate conditions for life through all of its parts -- health, fitness, and wellness. We are specifically looking at health and fitness in this book, but the same concepts can be applied to all areas of your life. Goal setting is essential to living your dream.

2

Behavior Change

Once you set a goal, the way to meet that goal is through changing your behaviors. This is where we go from self-awareness and analysis to the actual behavior change process. I like to use the transtheoretical model of behavior change as a broad way to look at this process. This model is integrative and dynamic. It allows each stage of change to be more fully understood, which gives us a greater ability to achieve the change we want. Everyone adheres to different programs based upon their interests, but no matter the program it is important that motivation, analysis, and behavior change become integral and applied together.

This specific model of behavior change is based on six phases. At any given time in your life you are in one of these phases. They apply to any and all behaviors, whether it's related to your career, finances, or even relationships. Have you ever realized that you perform the same activities (behaviors) day in and day out when it comes to any of these? Do those behaviors have the same result every time? Are you always chasing one goal the same way with the same result, whether it's success or failure?

Now is the time to step out of your comfort zone. It is time to self-analyze, self-motivate, and change those behaviors that do not work, replacing them with actions that will achieve your desired goal.

The first phase of behavior change is pre-contemplation. Pre-contemplation is when you come to the realization that something in your life could change but you may not see the value in that change. No matter how many times you do the same thing, you always get the same result. It could be a health risk, or a realization that you are on the path to a version of yourself that you do not want, but you do not see it. In this stage you are not taking action and you have no desire to take action.

Contemplation follows pre-contemplation. This is where the realization meets awareness. You could say pre-contemplation is walking through the woods and walking right into a spider web. Contemplation is when you are walking through the woods and step in a hole and break your leg. You can wipe the spider web off of your face, but that broken leg isn't as easy to fix. It's there to remind you that something is wrong. Now you have to figure out how you are going to tackle getting out of the woods with a broken leg.

The way to get out of the woods is to plan, which leads to the third phase: preparation. For some people, this transition happens when your clothes no longer fit and you have to buy a new wardrobe that is a size larger. Maybe you told yourself you would never wear a certain size, but now you have to. For others it might be the diagnosis of a chronic condition such as high blood pressure. These types of events can be especially eye opening if you told yourself you would never get to that point. If so, it is time to prepare to fix your behaviors and become a healthier and higher performing you. It is time to find out what you have to do to get out of the woods.

The most important thing you have to know is that life is the sum of its parts, and performance is achieved when all the pieces work in concert. Changing your unhealthy behaviors to healthy behaviors is one part of the equation, and the equation ends with optimization across the spectrum. Motivation can come from knowing where those unhealthy behaviors will take you and your loved ones, because again our life is a sum of its parts and the people in our life are included. What is the impact you have on your family and friends? What is the impact unhealthy behaviors have on your future? Use those impacts as a root of motivation to facilitate your change. Let them manifest into ideas of what you want to accomplish in your change.

When you do this you have to make a plan that lays out how you are going to make that idea or dream grow into a goal. This is the beginning of the planning process and the next phase, preparation.

Most people's fitness journeys are cut short because they have an idea of what they want to accomplish but they don't set the goal and plan up in a way that allows them to succeed. To use this stage to its full potential, your goal setting must work for you, not against you. In order to do this, use SMART goals. Goals that are:

Specific
Measurable
Attainable
Relevant
Time-bound

Too often people begin their fitness journey with the vague idea that they want to get into better shape. But what are they really working toward? A more specific goal, such as losing a number of pounds and inches, or being able to run a 5K, is measurable and sets the stage for success.

When setting your goals, first ask yourself some questions. How do you want to get in better shape? Do you want to improve your cardiovascular health? Do you want to become stronger? Do you want to become more powerful? Are you preparing for a special event, or hoping to look better for a special part of the year? Are you ready to change your behaviors to improve your overall health? Are you looking to set new personal records?

Use of the trans-theoretical model of behavior change and SMART goals apply to anyone for any progression. In fitness that covers the entire spectrum, from health to performance. Your goal might be going from a thirteen-inch bicep to a fifteen-inch bicep, or going from doing push-ups from the knee to push-ups from your feet. Maybe you are trying to outperform all your previous records. Or maybe you want to go from a sedentary lifestyle to an active lifestyle, or you want to go from just doing cardio to adding in strength training.

Goals even extend to nutrition, like going from unhealthy eating to becoming someone who prepares their healthful meals days before they eat them. These are all examples of transitions that can be made using behavior change and SMART goals. The accomplishment of any change, or goal in life, even beyond exercise and nutrition, can be made using this process and development of SMART goals.

Specific

Rather than a broad "I want to lose weight" or "I want to tone up," goals need to be targeted to set the stage for success. "I want to make my waist smaller." This example allows you to track your progress, because that goal is more specific than just toning up.

Measurable

Once you have set your goal for making your waist smaller, you have to ensure the goal is measurable and then get your baseline measurement. This allows you to keep track of your progress.

Attainable

Make your goal something you can accomplish, not something that is way out of reach. For this example, you might start with losing one inch off of your waist. One inch is attainable and you may even exceed it. Once you reach or exceed that goal, you can go from there. Let's compare a bad example. Many times people start with a general, non-specific goal of losing weight. With that weight-loss goal they throw a random number out there, let's say 30 pounds. They may even do this without considering what it will take to lose those 30 pounds. This is the opposite of attainable -- make sure the bar is not set too high. Motivation can be highly tied to progression towards a measurement, and you can set yourself up for success by making the goal attainable. Not to mention when you begin an exercise program you will begin to gain lean muscle which will have an impact on your total scale weight and may throw you off.

Relevant

Make the goal relevant to you. If the long-term goal is to improve your physique for swimsuit season, you must ask if the short-term goal of losing an inch off your waist line is relevant to that goal. Will it help you accomplish the long-term goal? In this case yes, but in some cases the goals we set don't take us to the place we want to be.

To explain this concept with the best detail, I must first distinguish between process and outcome goals. An outcome goal is the most common type of goal and provides a result, like losing an inch off your waistline or bench pressing a certain amount. The outcome goal is more closely related to long-term results. A process goal, on the other hand, is a goal that is tied more to the short-term actions that lead to the outcome goal. For example, a process goal would be going to the gym and training five days a week while adjusting nutrition, and an outcome would be improving physique by losing an inch off your waist.

The process goal must be relevant to the desired outcome. With a weight gain, weight loss, or any other desired outcome there must be alignment between process and outcome (relevance). For example, wanting to lose weight but having a process goal of going to the gym and training at a low intensity for only three days a week with no change in nutrition. Those process goals and outcomes are not in alignment and not relevant to each other. But, if you align them and make them relevant you are sure to see the outcome you desire.

Time-bound
Setting a date by when you will accomplish your goal keeps you accountable for doing what it takes to meet it. If you don't set a time-line you don't have anything keeping you accountable to perform the required work.

The SMART goal all boils down to knowing where you are starting and where you are going. If you don't know these things and you don't see your progress, you lose motivation. Not having a direction, accountability, or seeing how far you have come sets you up for failure. Failing to plan is planning to fail.

Losing inches off the waist is just one example. Any goals you have in mind can be reached using the SMART goal model. And remember, small goals are the key to accomplishing large goals. Just as waist reduction gets you to looking how you want to for swimsuit season, so does any short-term goal help you reach the long-term goal, if the goals are built correctly. In fact, the SMART goal keeps you motivated on that path because as you accomplish small goals (with one or two-week timelines) you are able to see your progress.

You should also translate the concept of small goals leading to large goals to how a process goal leads to an outcome goal. In the example I gave of losing weight, the process includes the intensity and frequency of training as well as nutrition; but all processes set the conditions for outcomes, just like you can set the conditions for your success. This is a concept you should continue to recognize day-to-day in order to achieve all the outcomes you want.

To circle back for a second, let's look again at keeping your goals attainable and time-bound. These parts of the SMART goal are important, but don't let that keep you from dreaming big. Make your goals big, make them challenging, and discover your potential by reaching them through structuring the process. If the long-term goal doesn't scare you then you aren't dreaming big enough.

Understanding how to build your goals gives you the ability to fully prepare to get out of the woods. Now you must take your preparation into the next phase, action. This can sometimes be the most difficult portion of behavior change. Your goals might look great on paper, but when you start acting on them you realize attainment may not be as easy as you thought. Staying motivated means keeping your goal in mind and knowing that you are on your way to accomplishing it. Keep the vision and trust the process.

During the action phase, it is important to track your progress. Accountability applies to doing the work as well as recognizing what you have already accomplished, in an efficient manner. For example, don't get fixed on the scale. It will only defeat you if you allow it to. Instead, track how much weight you are moving in a lift, how many reps you are performing, the distance you run, the pace, how your clothes fit, how you feel, or how you sleep. Then you will see that changes are being made and that you are on the way to the new, higher performing you. Acting on your goals is not easy, but it will pay off.

Action is not only the most difficult phase, it is the most dynamic. As you make improvements, your goals have to evolve to continue to challenge you.

Once you get to the point where you have met your goals and you are ready to maintain what you have accomplished, you have reached the next phase, maintenance. Some people never reach this phase, as they want to keep challenging themselves with new goals. But for those that do reach this phase in the exercise and fitness application, it is now time to manipulate your exercise program to maintain your fitness level.

Many people do this by changing the frequency, duration, or intensity of what they were doing during the action phase. You could increase the frequency, decrease the duration, and leave the intensity the same. For example, perform thirty minutes of exercise five times a week instead of ninety minutes three times a week. There are many ways to manipulate a program that will facilitate you maintaining your fitness level. The key is to find what you enjoy and what works for your scheduling.

The final phase is termination. This phase is reached when you cease to perform a behavior. Ideally you only want to terminate negative behaviors, like eating for stress relief, smoking, or shining a negative light on your perception.

In my experience, termination of a positive behavior like exercise is reached due to an injury, sickness, or other significant life event, but no matter what it is usually something negative impacting the positive. The important thing to know about termination in positive behaviors is that it can cause you to reduce your progress. If you reach termination of a positive behavior, the goal then becomes returning to the preparation phase once again to set the stage for your success.

Being able to adjust your goals based on your process is a key part of living your dream. Flexibility to the situation promotes long-term growth and progression.

Goal manipulation is the key to your behavior change and life-long advancement. If you do it for long enough, your behaviors will become part of your identity and they will be second nature to you. Your everyday activities will be those behaviors, and your life will be higher performing.

3

The Support System

Behavior change is dependent on your mindset. It is dependent on your ability to see the positive in a situation, your ability to be objective in a situation, and also your ability to be subjective and reward yourself with your emotions. All of these things are centralized around you as an individual, but while it's important to realize that you are the primary motivating factor, you don't have to go through your lifestyle changes alone.

Look around your world. Look at the people in it. Ask yourself this question: What is the common thing you recognize about the different people you see? I will bet you come up with an answer that sounds something like people are drawn to other people.

People are social creatures, just as most animals are. We like to be around other people. You may notice that most people, including yourself, have a set of close friends they rely on in addition to a large network of contacts.

Most people like being around other people. When life is worth celebrating we want to do it with the people we care about. But also, when life gets tough, it's nice to have a friend by your side. The common theme being we like to be around each other.

That brings us to the social aspect of your behaviors and behavior change — the support system. Creating a better version of yourself and establishing the conditions for optimal life performance can be overwhelming when relying on yourself.

What if you had one, three, five, or a community of friends to take the path with you? What if you fed off each other's positivity? What if you celebrated those victories with each other? What if you helped each other look at your behaviors analytically? How much easier would it be to pick the healthy food over the unhealthy one if you had someone doing it with you, keeping you accountable, and celebrating the choice together? What if you were there to pick each other up when you couldn't see any positivity?

The entire process of living a healthier and happier life only benefits by finding people to walk down the path of change with you. Not to mention this gives you the opportunity to meet new people, make new friendships, enhance old friendships, experience new things, and do them with people that are on the same road as you.

4

The Long Haul: Turning Motivation into Dedication

In today's world there are external motivations flying around everywhere. These are the things that promote you to want some type of tangible reward. It may be the envy that comes with seeing someone else's success or the motivation of seeing someone on their way to success, or even something as simple as a quote. External motivations have their place, but you can't forget about the motivations that live inside yourself, the intrinsic motivations. Those are the things that make you feel good, the things that make you happy and make you smile.

Are your motivations more driven by extrinsic or intrinsic roots? If you can find a way to be more intrinsically motivated, your journey will not only be more enjoyable, but it will also be something that you make a part of your everyday life, a part of your identity. You will look forward to doing the things that make you higher performing because they make you happy. For some it might be going to the gym for two hours a day. But it can be as simple as walking in the park with your dog or your friends. It can be lifting, training, biking, walking, running, exploring, hiking, or finding new activities to do with your friends. If you enjoy the social environment and that is where you find yourself the happiest, change up what your friends do. Plan a hiking trip rather than meeting for lunch. Become active with that same group of people.

Once you find what you enjoy, you must tie your motivation to that. If you can combine those things, you can turn motivation into dedication. If you use that dedication to build your goals, you can have a system that will always be there to keep you going; to keep you in the action and maintenance phases.

If you don't know what type of activity or activities you really enjoy, you need to find out by exploring some options. Your comfort zone is not the best place to be. If you want your lifestyle change to work you are going to have to try new things. Think outside of your normal box. That is not to say you need to overwhelm yourself, but you certainly need to provide a challenge. Look at your current lifestyle and what you enjoy doing. Are there any activities or interests that can be carried into exercise in any way? Are there any exercise methods that you are interested in trying?

The biggest goal for those in a sedentary lifestyle is to increase the overall activity level. If you are just starting off, that doesn't mean you have to immediately start an exhausting exercise program. Look for ways you can increase your activity in your everyday life. Park at the back of the parking lot, use the stairs, go the long way to your office, use an activity tracker to prompt you to get up and move during the day. These are the types of things that will lead to more activity and more positive choices. They will motivate you to find new ways to increase your activity. Eventually you will be in the gym, on the track, on a lifting platform, or on a hiking path regularly. Find what makes you happy and let those things drive you to do more. Let those things become habits and turn your motivation into dedication.

5

Habits of Performance

When I hear the word habit it makes me think of an action, something that someone does as a part of their normal routine. The word routine brings up the idea that we as humans are creatures of habit. These words ultimately live in association with each other. One follows the other in a cyclical fashion.

I have found there are different types of people: those that have habits of success and performance and those that do not. This may sound a little simplistic, but that is what I am showing in this book. Using a model of behavior change and SMART goals in any pursuit of self-improvement is simple, but life-changing.

Your life is the sum of its parts, and that means all the things you do (behaviors and routines) are ultimately who you are. This is a philosophy, that actions determine results. Actions are your intentions and a reflection of who you are deep down. What you do behind closed doors and what you do out in the world all give a look into what type of person you are, words alone are irrelevant.

With that said, habits are the repetition of actions, and anyone has the ability to change their actions. In the words of Aristotle, "We are what we repeatedly do. Excellence, then, is not an act but a habit." We all have the ability to be high performing persons by changing our actions and habits.

Action, persistence, consistency, analyzation, determination, positivity, and flexibility: these words describe the steps of creating the habitation of what I believe to be successful routines. If you allow your environment to influence you there is a possibility you will remain in your current routine, or worse. But using these steps gives you the ability to turn your current habits and routine into that of performance, or enhance upon what you already do.

My general rule for defining the habits of performance are that they are centralized around doing what must be done and being disciplined. Some people seem to be born with the natural, innate characteristics of this, but even if it takes work for you, the effort you put into it can be more powerful than you would ever imagine.

Any area of life can benefit from goal setting and action. Let's explore this in the example of a workout program. If you were to download an exercise program that is written and posted online for everyone, I would bet you don't get the same result that everyone else does. If you put more in you get more out. On the other hand you could have the best exercise session ever designed just for you, but if you don't put the effort in you will not get your return on that investment in your body, no matter who you are. The same concept applies to all areas of life progression.

This effort and discipline on those efforts are key to seeing results in the change or enhancement of your actions, habits, and behaviors. Discipline in everything you do is needed to obtain what you are seeking. So far, we have hard work (effort) and discipline. The next piece of success is the ability to always have the goal in mind. The goal and end result are crucial, losing sight of that is what many times will limit a person's progression. Seeing the goal at the end, no matter the situation, sets those that succeed apart from those that do not. If you lose sight of the goal then you can drown in the day-to-day distractions.

Discipline, hard work, and keeping the goal in sight are my definition of habits of performance. Through this book, I hope to have given you the tools to decide and determine what your habits need to be in order for you to create your success.

I know that success does not have a singular definition. I know that each facet of life is very dynamic and requires an individualized approach that at many times an outsider has no way of understanding. The key to success is creating it yourself through actions and habits. Now you must ask yourself, what are your current routines leading you towards, and are there changes that need to be or could be made so that you are successful, by your definition? You have to use your ability to build an effective goal and analyze your behaviors, and then use discipline, hard work, and sight of that goal to create the future you desire.

The foundation of a high-performance life is rooted in a healthy body and mind. Using your analytics to self-assess where you stand in comparison to where you dream to stand is key to building the conditions for that performance. Next you must be able to turn that dream into long and short-term goals that facilitate your progression and use your behaviors to your advantage. In this book I have mostly applied these concepts to exercise and health, but they are applicable to every piece of your life. Develop a foundation of health in your body and mind so you may see its manifestation of performance in everything you do, from your family life to your career to your finances.

www.ingramcontent.com/pod-product-compliance
Lightning Source LLC
Chambersburg PA
CBHW031516210526
45464CB00007B/2942